Soundings
Poems and Essays

Rich Katims

Asoka Press
Stone Ridge, NY

Published by the Asoka Press,
P.O. Box 46, Stone Ridge, NY 12484
Copyright © 1999, Rich Katims
ISBN 0-9676259-0-4

This book was designed and produced by Ide Katims, Ph.D.

All proceeds from the sale of this book go to the Ulster
Community College Foundation Dr. Richard Katims Scholarship
Fund.

This book is dedicated to my family:
Sam, Rita, Joel, Ide and Ren

CONTENTS

II ESSAYS

Introduction

Soundings is a select collection of my poems and essays written over the past several years. If you are surprised by its creation, this may be because many of you have known me primarily as a professor of political science at Ulster County Community College, where I have been teaching since 1969. Or at least as a presence on area tennis courts.

I don't typically write political poems, and only occasionally do political images appear in my poems. But for me, however, there are key intersections--not always obvious--among the political, the poetic and the cultural. Writing poems, for example, is a good way of digging deeply not only into what my own psyche or consciousness may reveal, but also to the roots of culture.

To teach and create poetry and essays give what we call "voice" to a multiplicity of ideas, images and other forms of deep expression. Ulster County Poet Laureate Bob Steuding defined voice as "the evocation, even the epiphany of self. Voice emerges from and gives shape to genuine life experience." *Soundings* is really a reflection of my search for and finding a voice--an expression of the multiple beings who make me up. This is what I want to share with you, especially the poetry (the essays much more concern our collective voices). I have presented the poems in an order not so much to show their thematic or stylistic similarity, but to prompt you to pause and ask "what was he doing, thinking, feeling when he wrote that?"; "how do the poems show the various facets of his life, particularly as family member; teacher; athlete; spiritual practitioner; political and social activist; traveler and friend?"

Some of the poems and essays have been previously published individually or have been anthologized; some have been re-written or revised for inclusion in *Soundings*. You may also notice that some images appear more than once, in various contexts, and that on occasion I use quoted lines from other poets or writers (Basho, Snyder, Shantideva). I hope you will see this as a kind of creative recycling rather than lack of imagination.

I also hope you enjoy reading *Soundings* as much as I have writing and living it.

Rich Katims
Ulster County Community College
Stone Ridge, New York

1

Poems

Awakenings

The desert is a whispering place where
iron illusions of stillness silence
hot-blooded trees ablaze with twilight screams;
the sky darkens in waves.

Dinosaur cliffs rise up, pulsing, frozen by
night-chilled winds; stars break clear
of the moon's tide-cooled light, hidden at first
by the thinnest veil of mind, appearing now

not because the sky grows darker,
but because one grows more awake.
In the glow of the morning sun the

Chiricahua mountains, like spiral drippings
from a child's pail, mirror the silent,
squatting old-honed tribal
men tucked behind tough leather eyes:

a geological council of elders; fine dust forms
in the folds of weathered, igneous brows;
the Ancient Ones sit, wait and answer in one voice.

Along The Shore

Late afternoon. When you left
I walked along the shore.
Old folks fished in low-tide surf.
Sandpipers glided in a sea-foam bath.
Seagulls pierced the evening fog:
Caw-cophony of mist-tipped wings.
A heron's gaze reflected the
Setting sun. I wrote your name
In the sand and said good-bye.

Movements

In Berkeley, brush-cut punks draped in snakes
and cracked-leather smiles picket the air waves
for ignoring their songs. "The sixties are dead,"
they rail against the tone-deaf brick, "Sid Vicious
has died for your sins."

I walk the streets mourning my lost twenties
and think of my old friend, sad-eyed Terri,
who in our time of lawyers and shrinks,
wanted to come to the coast to study rocks and bones.

But we all laughed, so she married an Italian jeweler
with three kids and had three more.

I have come to hunt the ghost of Mario Savio,
but outside Sproul Hall they talk of earthquakes
and other more recent movements, while
Hare Krishnas jingle and drum away bad vibes.

A kid on a skateboard, like a black comet
on wheels, weaves through the crowd,
leaps above the streets, then fizzles in the Bay,
the smoke from his sizzling tail melts into
the fog drifting in, slowly, from the west.

Thaws

*("The Chinese seem to realize that their unprecedented
journey to the U.S. means they are entering the age of high
tech. Not only have they come here to establish an accord
with the U.S. but to show their people back home what
"modernization" is all about. As a result, they are paying
scrupulous attention to every public detail of their sojourn
as the first televised reflections of America are beamed back
to China" --Orville Schell, "Watch Out for the Foreign
Guests," 1981)*

Roads clear, heels dig in soft snow-crust;
winter, that vengeful, arthritic tyrant,
rolls on its side and groans; a
phantom, low-in-the-sky sun
sneaks in and skids East to West
normalizing, balancing power:

China cashing in revolutionary red chips
for IBM blue, splashing
posters of Mao with Coca-Cola
and genuine, Texas store-bought bull sperm,
while ice jams the watercourse way.

This chiseled, crystal time hardens
and packs me down,
crouching stiff within myself
behind a sharp-edged, wind-shaped shell.

On Mohonk Mountain, the snapping
cracks in rocks wend
a steady path up my leg,
through my brain, and down the other side.

Stormwatch

Watching the storm from the inside:
crashing through the woods it
snaps the limbs of trees
slips through cracks in doors
makes me hide in books.

Ide sleeps--her face locked
in a battle we avoid;
it is the Chinese New Year's Eve;
the snake must slink away
in the snow or fight

the mustang's slashing hooves;
a good time, they say, for
business confidence (taking stock);
put some grease on my boots
turn my back to the wind

get ready to dig out.

Prisons

Sitting on a Minnewaska ledge:
below, the sheer cliff joins bare trees,
flowing into each other;
a thickening mist shrouds the valley
deep into my mind.

Dry leaves rattle on December scrub oak;
the wind fills my head
and stops
the roar of an oil truck
winding up the mountain road.

Across the granite outcrop,
a soft-spoken black man behind bars,
once a hired killer of
other men, waits ten
thousand lifetimes for me to come--

to give him what I do not yet have:
the wisdom to see that "buddhas work for the
benefit of others;" and the truth for us
is that there is only this winding mountain road

on which the F.B.I. came to our Woodstock door
for leads to capture the soft-voiced killer
on the loose, who murdered again,
and the truth for us lays shrouded
like a thickening mist deep into our minds.

Thieves
(for Jack)

I

When you were fifteen
you'd steal a bicycle and
from the saddle
shoot out warehouse windows
with an old twenty-two,
then hop the freight train and
ride like a hobo through town
until they'd come and
take you to the judge, who
wore white socks and a vodka grin
and once again they'd send
you home, such as it was.

Out back your mama grew okra
and collard greens,
while upstairs that man
you called your father
but wasn't
grew hard with your sister,
who was ten. Even then

your arms were steel bands
wrapped around bone, and
though you smiled
like the day was yours,
your eyes were fiery pits
stoked by rage, blowing inside
like a great bellows;

and everywhere you saw snakes.

But you could draw like Michelangelo:
dreamworld beings who could
fly and slither off the page,
singe your hair from fifty feet,
change your blood to steam
make you turn your eyes.

And so twenty years ago
I wrote this poem for you:

II

Shaman Song for Jack:
the slit-eyed, slime-scaled dragon
churning the shrouded sea,
and the bronze-winged
talon-toed womanbird leaping
from the mountain's edge
the golden-robed samurai
        are you
crush their bones, chew their veins
dance lightly and pray

III

Now when I see the
headline, small as it is,
"homeless man caught in bicycle theft,"
I know it is you.

And there you are:
hollow eyes shot out,
your smile a twisted curl

of withered rope,
arms tracked for hobo trains
snaking the back alleys of
some town you inhabit alone.

And here am I:
picking dragon veins from my teeth
with shards of shaman bones
dancing talon-toed, golden-robed
at the mountain's edge
waiting for you, waiting
like you, to leap.

Passages
(for Bob Steuding)

Back at your house, after climbing the cliffs
of South Mountain still again, I sneak off
to the den to breathe the clean smell
of new books and "real work" on the desk.

Wives (this time) chop the tomatoes and cheese.
Rice steams on the wood stove; the old Riteway
warms the kitchen chill. Your little guy Miles,
and Bill, taking time off from being
an outlaw in New Mexico, carry in the logs.

Food and talk pass around the table; minds and
stomachs churn and chew as one. We celebrate
the Buddha, the dharma and the sangha, but we know
the rituals are these times together, venerating *each other*.

Yes, this life is shadow-streaked with pain;
we suffer for eons past, lifetimes not yet lived.
But Shantideva teaches, "whatever is the source
of pain and suffering, let that be the object of our fear."

So I watch you, my bodhisattva brother, as teacher,
father and love mate, "cultivate the ocean like immensity
of joy arising when all beings will be freed,
acting for others' sake, guarding and shielding them
with compassion," living the enlightened heart of bodhicitta.

And perhaps one day we will smile again in the full glow of
"the dawning moon of the mind," coming down the
rockslide on Friday Mountain, knowing your sheep's whole,
safe trip has been in the barn--and soon we'll eat her, too.

Big Sur

At Pfeiffer Beach I read Jeffers
    to learn about
    Big Sur, but

The roaring surf and morning sun
    glinting from a
    sea-carved cliff
                distract me

And just over my shoulder
    a spotted lizard
    scratches in the brush.

The wind gusts in sandy swirls;
    by tomorrow
    I'd be covered.

Perhaps a night heron will
    build a nest
    in my hair and

Use a tattered book to shield
    the fragile eggs
    that bear her young.

The Inner "I"
(for Jonathan Kozol)

They watched you circle slowly,
your hook-beak silhouette
against the growling clouds,
expecting a vulture to come
to pick the carcass of America,
a covey of golden rings
gleaming on fat-caked claws.

But you came as an eagle--
in wing-tipped shoes looking
more like a rabbi than Che Guevara--
striking sure and swift,
thinning a herd grown weak
from the wounds of half-lived lives;

bringing the Word; opening the inner "I";
then soaring back: the filling moon
splits a coal-streaked sky,
Catskill foothills just beyond reach.

The Good Life

Ide:
>lying
>eyes closed
>in bed
>eating
>sweet red grapes;
>her after-bath
>freckled
>Chinese face
>at peace
>
>(life is
>sometimes
>not so bad)

Back Home

Back home, near the top
High Point Mountain
bristles in the cold December wind.
Just south
where the hemlock come back,
the great whale Mombacus
throbs to the wingbeat of hawks.

Scrub oak fire
pot of strong mu tea:
warm our bones
soothe our aches
melt our screams
at the meadow's edge.

Watching the weather
talking our minds to death
listening for deer

we *live* among these hills.

San Francisco

Chinatown

In Chinatown, the "box man" decked in
paper bag hat and rice sack boots
drags his urine-soaked soul
along tourist-clogged streets, a wake
of empty cartons bobs drunkenly behind him
like life on a short string. When he

dies they'll stuff him harshly in his
most prized box, the one with the address
still marked, the one that brought all
those bronze buddhas from Hong Kong,
the one big box marked "fragile."

They'll mail him right back to the street
and they'll wonder about the smell,
the god-awful smell, they'll be sure to ask
about the smell coming from the box
marked "Fragile, 50 Buddhas." In Chinatown,

Ah Gung and his grandchildren eat dim sum
without a word. He reads his newspaper,
the kids eye the clock on the golden-dragon wall;
he pays the check and sighs as they
scoot out the door, their new Adidas sneakers
bolting further West than his fading eyes can see.

Orpheus Downtown

On Market and Powell the telephone troubadour,
a white-afro'd Orpheus in overalls,
serenades his reflection in the shiny glass booth,

while Eurydice waits underground, in the BART,
making small talk with Hades at the crossroads,
waiting for the sun to shine, his shadow to fade.

Tremors

Outside Old St. Mary's, on the stoop,
wearing knitted hat and lumberjack shirt,
she asks for quarters, catching the camera-strung,
street-car crowd at noon; but it's her voice,
her terrible voice, that gets them:

"Spaaare your chaaange?," she whines,
then mumbles some secret ancient runes,
curses that burn your groin, singe your hair.
My quarter is *always* ready; when the
"big one" comes, I"ll not bear the blame.

Grant Avenue Neap Tide

From the window of my landlocked room,
I can hear the pulsing stream of cars
whooshing through busy downtown streets;
they sound like sea-waves pounding
the beach of a distant coral shore.

I close my eyes and see coffee-skinned
women bathing naked in the surf,
the lines of great poems coiled in the
curves of their salt-tipped breasts.

The tide comes in on Grant Avenue below;
a bus sets sail for ports unknown.

North Beach

In Washington Square, at dusk,
an old wino in rags picks
his supper from the garbaged ruins
of Sunday family feasts,
a green toe like an old frog
gapes from his one shit-stained shoe

held together with string. The church
bells gracing the park gong
on the hour; it is six o'clock. I check
my watch, place my book in my pack,
get ready to leave,
looking as if there *is* somewhere to go.

Atonements

On Yom Kippur, in primal silence,
I walk again with Ezra, Daniel and Enoch
on Guardian Mountain, overlooking Woodstock.

One thing I know: there is a
deep grammar of love, a nucleoplasmic
remembering, cell by cell, of
some cretaceous dance among ferns

syntax of smell, pulsing heat
searing in and out; bone to bone,
breath to breath, claw to claw

the silent stare of my baby feeding late
in the night, tiny fingers locked on my thumb
I promised him the time of his life

the mind pouring itself like lava
a molten sea of names and stories
"mountains and rivers without end"

forgetting is the affliction of the soul:
forgive me for the sins I have sinned
for the souls that I have saved
absolve me of all vows

Kol nidre.

Descents

Leaping from rock to log:
our *bodies* know the way down.
Bob and Bill on the ridge below
step over the lip of space, then vanish
like hawks hunting in the sun.

We stop by a stream: blown beards
drip with cold clear delight.
Skipping and sliding on rubber legs,
our thoughts our own, someone shouts
"Hey, I can go ten more miles."

We get to the truck (old pasture horse not
quite where it was), waiting to take us back.
Riding snug and calm, I think of my lady
at home, by the fire, sipping wine.

Bearded Jews

My beard reminds my father
of *his* father who
as a Jew
with a beard
was thrown down and stoned
in the old neighborhood.

My father says: "how I hated him
with a beard because
they knew, even from afar,
he was a Jew."

Now my father hates *me*
with a beard
and throws stones when
I come home
because, even from afar,
I look too much
like his father, a Jew.

Ten-Cord Winter

Here it is already spring, redwings back,
opening day just two weeks off,
but out of the vernal shadow, in the
purple glow of the filling moon:
still *another* snow. Watching the storm

from the inside, I sit in the midnight stillness,
close to the stove, listening to
the crack and sizzle of seasoned wood:
fine-grained ash, burn it green, gives hot coals;
solid oak from tough old stock; hickory logs
heavy as stones, make the house smell good.

This year: seven feet of snow in a ten-cord winter
that nearly froze us to the bones.
At thirty below, these bones creak and snap
like roof beams pulling in on themselves
in the night. Just past dawn the winter sun
cuts through the trees like a sword;

things so clear you want to cry, new snow knee-deep,
and for awhile no road: just trees and fields,
the frozen pond, a barn, neighbors across
the stream warm in houses tucked among hills:
all of us sharing "this living, flowing land."

Then the raucous call of crows and hum of the
bearded boys with plows piloting four-wheeled scows,
crashing through snow waves like
sea captains along some great barrier drift--
they've come to dig us out. All winter

Ren and I rode the Mississippi with Jim and Huck,
rooting out rattlers, pressing our luck,
our raft a sled, outracing dark forces lurking
under the bed; some Indians say, "the best storyteller
is one who lets you live if the weather is bad."

Stories are told on winter nights, the grammar of things:
molecules of large truths held still enough to watch,
as if spun by some quantum magic from secrets
locked in crystal shards of space caught in time:
the mind's frozen stare looking back at itself;
nothing to see, really, but the light of the filling moon,
winking eye of the storm, fire cracking in the stove.

Soon I will lie by the pond in late April grass,
like a snake, flicking my tongue at new-hatched flies;
the sun will warm these bones, color my face like a mask.
I will listen to the wind in the trees, then reach out,
cup my hands, and drink from the still-cold water of
the ten-cord winter that nearly froze us to the bones.

Dancing Face Of Love
(for Jay and Joan Neuhoff)

Here I am: a thousand years old,
dreaming again the jagged dreams that
pierced my skin like golden thorns,
and the blood flowed hot as lava
melting rocks, burning trees,

And I would cup that blood in my
hands as if it were a great clear pond,
then watch the world rise and set,
darkness unto light, my mother of Mothers,
seeing forever the dancing face of love.

Lime Hill

Looking beyond a sun-streaked field, I see a lime hill and, for a moment, think it has snowed. But it is Indian summer, early November, and the "pock-pock" of tennis balls rockets through the gold-tipped air. Lucie and I watch and listen for the wing beat of Canada geese in drunken lines of twelve, then walk through unploughed rows of rope-tough corn like hunters stalking the giant winter bear. Beneath this teasing warmth, this rainbow'd time, Autumn, like a beautiful goddess with a cold heart, chills me to the bone, giving and taking at will. At home, growing warm by the fire, Ren ponders why the geese fly off while, after all these years, I still shake with the wonder of why that lady's diamond heart makes me suffer so.

Soundings

("We dive and reappear in new places."--Emerson)

At dusk among the songs of the *outside*--
the wingbeat of a heron lifting
from the pond, love call of
bullfrogs through the twilight mist--
I sit listening to the sounds *inside*:

the clicking of chopsticks as
a Chinese woman, my wife
sizzling stir fry on the stove;
a laughing boy, my son
feeding tortilla chips to his dog;
the neighbor's kid across the stream
blowing Charlie Parker riffs on his sax.

Here along the jagged seam of night and day,
where things turn inside out,
I could disappear: crawl out of my skin
like a snake and leave it on a fencepost
to blow like a kite in the evening breeze;
or move downstream with the beaver,
build new ponds, eat the bark of trees.

The boy calls, the dog howls.
I come home and smell the steaming food.
The woman smiles. We eat quietly
among the sounds outside:

the beebop love song of bullfrogs,
whisper-walk of heron,
startled splash of beaver in the pond
Living inside and out,
diving and reappearing in new places.

Sons

("Brothers, 3 and 5, Killed In Snowmobile
Mishap"--Daily Freeman)

In the morning of the first big snow,
a year after your sons have died,
I walk towards your house,

my son Ren cradled in my arms,
swaddled in brown, snub nose running;
deer tracks cross the frozen pond.

Through your basement window I see
a folded crib pressed like cell bars against
the ice-streaked glass. Then, ever so gently

I raise my boy: round-eyed wonder in his face,
tiny hands tucked into the folds of my coat, cold,
sweet breath on my cheek. As softly as my heart

will allow, for the new year, amid the swirling snow,
in the winter shadow of your house and the primal
power of our shared paternal love,
I hold my son with you.

Phases

(*"beautiful from the heart"--Ninba: Nepal*

*"In 1992 there was such widespread famine
in Africa that millions faced death by starvation.
In Somalia there was a civil war and the country
was near anarchy. Warring factions stole
emergency food to feed the hungry."--United Nations)*

I

Now in early December
the light of the hunter moon
splinters and cracks on the ice-crusted pond.
I look for your face,
listen for your voice among the
silver branches of maple and spruce;

but in the clear frozen night:
I hear the sparrow-call of
far-away children, eyes like full moons
in sunken black faces covered with flies,
arms and legs like twigs.
A screech owl swoops from a distant pine.

II

The smell of gunshot fades;
deer snort and drink
from a spring in the shadow of woods
close to the pond. I look for you again among
the trees remembering when
the full moon burst

through the late-summer mist
like a one-eyed ghost and lit your face like a jewel.
The children were silent then;
your voice was a song in the night
and it was beautiful from the heart.
In the still point of dreams I fly with golden eagles.

Ren's Poem

When I was a bird
eating seeds,
I lived on the water with fish
and high on the mountaintops
where clouds hid my nest.

When I was a flower
dancing with bees,
I raised my face to the sun,
put my back to the rain
and turned into a boy

who chases the wind.
Daytime sinks into the forest;
three deer drink from the pond;
the moon is hiding in the trees;
when will Mommy be home?

Returns

This summer the pond is thick and wild; at the edge:
willowherbs, meadowsweet, a stand of yellow flag.
Knee-deep in sedge I watch a grass snake wind through
tall bur-reeds, while a big brown turtle floats in the sun
like a great snouted stone, afraid of nothing.

And now slowly, slowly, the pond is filling in.
Where once I dove deep beneath lilies and spied
from below the circle dance of dragonflies blue with lust,
I stand tall on layers of leaves and silt, the wash of
last spring's storms, detritus of things left undone.

But when the pond goes back to maple and fern,
what will become of the once-shy woman-girl
who lives under the water,
surrounded by bass and perch, the green glow of algae,
a nest of twigs in the curls of her matted hair?

Will she go downstream with the beaver, build new dams,
shine her honey-woman smile at some careless boy or
a handsome young bear stoned on berries and grubs?
Or will she turn into a willow tree and call
once more on moonless winter nights to howl as one in

the frozen wind, climb naked on her dagger spine,
skin peeled back like bark, blood running like sap?
And then who will come to hear her speak the names,
whisper the stories, a hint of lilac on her breath,
together watching the eyes of deer turn into stars?

Curves

On Halloween eve
by the pond
the last waterstriders,
dressed as themselves,
skate the surface
thinking God knows what.

Ren leaps from the bus,
sees mallard mates
gliding in the tall reeds
and asks, what lives in
Transylvania and has webbed feet?
I give up, what? Count Duckula!

The air is still warm,
and this is a baseball poem,
so we grab our gear:
strange shiny aluminum bat,
grass-stained ball, cow-hide
gloves, well-oiled and soft.

Ren shakes off the sign,
then windmill winds
like Satchell in his prime;
Thwock! Struck me out
again: three up,
three down, nothing across.

At bat, he points to center field
like the Babe in Chicago, 1932
then belts one
over the split rail fence,
and does a slow jog
around the yard.

I showed my boy how,
told the stories, spoke the names;
but can I teach him to love,
to hold this life
across the seams, spinning along
the light-lines of this Earth?

Soon it will be winter.
The pond will turn to ice;
snow will cover
the frozen fields,
and we will know again
who lives with us.

Paths

("None to accompany me on this path: Nightfall in Autumn"--Basho)

Late Autumn; the days snap shut. I hear the far-off hum
of chainsaws: woodpiles build beneath open-shed roofs.
The grass glows white in early-morning frost.
A doe and fawn graze in the meadow close to our house,
growing fat for winter or city hunter's whiskey-cocked gun.

In South Hollow, the stream is high. I climb to the cliffs
through past-bloom mountain laurel and shaggy hemlock,
the sweet scent of a thousand hikes wafting from my pack.
My bones suck in the wild things here: the smell of bear,
dream songs sung, love talk spoken low.

The sun drops behind High Point's western ridge. In the
evening chill, I brew strong green tea, then watch the smoke
rise from the roof of a cabin in the ice-carved valley below.
Inside, people come together by the fire; but here on these
sandstone rocks, in late Autumn, I am on this path all alone.

Hong Kong

Float into Kai Tak:
big DC-10
swallowed by Kowloon;
hot mist like dragon breath
hangs over Victoria Peak.

In the South China Sea
junk boats
billow bravely on
white-capped water home.

Ide, though thick with America,
rolls in a black-haired
slim-hipped sea;
she is my tongue,

I am odd-man out;
my bearded, long-nosed strangeness
grinds in the swell and press
of millions of people

Swarming in steambath streets,
air-drill roar,
mah-jongg clack,
the smell of dried salt fish

and jingle of cold, hard cash.

Heroes

I

They search for signs of heroes
Probing the black cracks in trees,
Watching sea-bound sails for the
Mark of magic winds, seeing
Miracle births in the
Swaying tendrils of clouds.

At dusk the day splits along a
Hidden jagged seam; dusk-dancers
Glide and sing forbidden
Songs of ancient kings.

II

I watch her chase the Church Street
Bus, a ragged black cello case
Pressed beneath one sparrow-arm,
The other waves a blind man's stick
Scraping ghost-white arcs
Across the concrete path; then

She boards the bus and
Melts into the sour smell of
A thousand other everyday folks
Coming home from work.

Forms
(for Tom Davis)

Sitting on the back porch steps in late April sun, new Feng Shui wind chimes ringing overhead, the smoke of Kosovo, a Balkan shadow blowing by, I see the white painted markings on the red maple under which I buried our cats who died of things cats sometimes do, but needn't. Katie turned out to be a male, and Max a girl, but in the end it hardly mattered. We couldn't seem to keep cats, all the others were run off by the neighbors' orange tom who'd come and stomp right up to their bowl, take their food, stare, hiss and march off like a lion to their seeming eternal kittenhood.

After many years of sitting on that porch, scanning those woods, I realize I miss those cats, not for their love or friendship--they came for food not comradery--but because of how they'd steal like leopards through the tall grass by the pond; swatting at dragon flies and clover-drunk bees, watching for mice, spitting back at snakes; or suddenly appearing from odd angles, like cat ghosts, leaping like ancient Olympians from high hidden places to brush my arm, lick my sweaty hand with sand paper tongue.

Sitting on that porch, I wonder about that aging orange tom and how he must now fight for food without much grace or wit with the neighbors' new young toughs. When he dies, will they bury him under a nearby tree, or scatter his ashes in the wind, as mine soon will be, or will he be sucked into some vet's packed black hole, a platonic grave of Persians, Maine Coons, and Siamese and who, all mixed together, finally explain, after all this time, the real essence of pure perfect philosophical Forms--the ones who may or may not stink if there's nobody around to smell them rot in the forest, and who certainly would give no concern for plunging into that ever-changing Heraclitean river, no matter the heat of the grave or the once-fearsome power of that leonine orange tom?

Practice

Thoughts:

move faster than breath,
magical barbed golden arrows
scatter cooing pigeons who
nest in the roof; thoughts

roll past in little red-wrapped
boxes with curled bows
addressed to me
a gift, the present, now

the guy next to me sitting,
sleeping on his Alan Watts
autograph model *zafu*
bobs and nods (rising, falling

rising, falling) like a clay duck
decoy from a hunter's blind;
or maybe he's *davening*:
better to pay it no-Mind.

Pulse

sliding *past* the Mother now

your mouth, the wind,
the swirl of life beyond
the blood of birth
filling tiny lungs with air.

wrinkled little body
racked with the will
to *live*
to dance upon this earth
filling space

we are *all* one breath.

Thresholds

Coming down Tremper Mountain, near the stream,
in the fractured light of early summer sun,
there was a bear: Black Anu or Artemis of the Moon
gliding through the trees, "leaping from
rock to log," calling across the threshold
like a shadow behind the eyes; then gone.

Last spring, as the great snow melt covered
the bare bones of the Ashokan, I sat in
the same tall grass along the riprap dam
watching the water roar and foam fly,
the splash of fish joy near the shore.
I whispered in the wind: there *is* a god.

Then in summer I put in a garden, an offering,
not much more than a large salad: lettuce,
cucumbers, green peppers, tomatoes and beans.
I weeded and watered, and watched them grow with
the wide eyes of a child; but so did the deer
who came one moonless night and ate it all.

This year, no garden, but coming up from the compost
(wood ash, grass, banana peels, egg shells):
a wild zucchini, yellow flowers tucked into
themselves like shy children, then flared like
dancing girls, broad leaves studded with morning dew,
winding along the shed with great dignity and purpose.

Each day now, by the pond, I watch sunfish (the males)
like sentries guard their nests. I stop
and salute in dorsal recognition, some show
of paternal solidarity, but they only stare back
and scowl, as if to scold me for leaving my eggs,
and when I swim they come and nip my toes. Our

Lives are prey to bass and perch, the cool currents
of underground springs, scars of things left undone,
call of the she-bear from moon shadows behind the eyes;
never hearing the stories, speaking the names, or
running with wildflowers knee-deep in late summer;
and knowing in silence the cytoplasmic dance of love.

Hunters

(for Jeffrey and Amy Katims)

He wears a cardboard rabbit
tied around his neck with yarn
that says he's Ricky Chu and
to please return him if he's gone.

Ricky wields a plastic shovel longer
than his arm, and leads a troop of hunters
who chase pigeons in the park.
"Yaaaiii," he screams, running with delight,

his gleaming, round, laughing face
squeezing almond-eyes shut tight.
I long to take him by the hand,
lick his sticky ice-pop fingers clean;

instead, I ask him, "Ricky Chu, do hunters
ever lose their way?" He answers:
"No, lost is just another way to play,
but sometimes cardboard rabbits do."

Tao Te Ching
Chapter XXXII
(A translation for Ren, Joshua and Raphaela)

The way of life's natural flow is forever
and has no name
Even at its simplest there is
nothing to hold onto
All powerful attempts to harness it
are in vain
Knowing this, things take their normal course
Heaven and earth are joined
and we are cleansed by soft falling rain

Joining in the way of life's natural flow
with no need to name this or that
is to experience all things as one
And so the stream runs to the river
and the river flows home to the sea

Journey

("Sentient beings are as limitless as the whole of space:
May they each effortlessly realize the nature of their
mind..."--Shantideva, The Way of the Bodhisattva)

Seven hundred days I have
walked these shadowed trails
over a thousand mountains,
singing with each step.
My legs move now on their own;
often I forget where I've been
and where I am bound. My wife,
dead these many years,
walked for months beside me
made tea from lotus roots,
then stopped to rest in a
forest house we built from
mountain mist and youthful dreams.

In three hundred days more
I will come to the Temple of
Yellow Plum Mountain.
What will I know?
At night the forest is
so cold; my bones are like
frozen oak. Still I walk in
the ancient, silent steps of the
others before me: together
we walk the path of Mind.

Today, as for the past eight days,
I will take no food or drink.
I chant and watch and listen.
In the morning I will carry water
to the Buddha. From this bare
wooden room I smell the water in

the distant well. I can hear
ashes dropping from incense sticks
in the far temple hall. I watch
the air shimmer in a great blue void
and see the colors of wind
disperse around clacking bamboo chimes.

The world falls through my eyes.
Now my skin hangs like an empty
cracking sack on these ancient iron bones.
My veins are knotted strings;
I float in faintly pulsing blood,
bobbing gently through my heart,
such a pure and perfect carved canyon.

No matter. Today is the ninth day.
Tomorrow I will sip warm green tea;
they will call me *ah ja-ri*, great teacher
and sage. What is there to know?
In the morning I will carry the Buddha
to the well, drink my fill, and be on my way.

2
Essays

The Power Within, The Power Without:
Toward An Integration of Spiritual and Social Action

"Power is only insight into the void--the single thought that illuminates the heart."[1]

I teach political philosophy in a small, upstate-New York community college. While for most students, the course is a first real involvement with the ideas I raise and the thinkers we read, I assign a rather difficult final undertaking: to crystalize what they perceive to be the most important or intriguing question political theory should be dealing with right now, and describe how that question touches the core of their lives. Hoping to make their time easier, I suggest how I would approach the assignment. Here is what I say:

Of fundamental importance in my life right now (and, in fact, for the past 25 years) is a quest for what might be called "spiritual understanding." I have come to see that this concern involves a meditative path which I hope will lead to a greater awakening in me of compassion and wisdom. At the same time, however, I am deeply involved with the political questions of our time and, through teaching and other forms of participation, I have taken an activist, even radical stance--especially regarding civil rights, war, and poverty. I wonder how to reconcile the more meditative and activist parts of my life and how they might either complement or contradict each other (or both).

Thus, are spiritual and social activism incompatible: Can the "power within" be integrated with the "power without?" The discussion that follows is a deeper exploration, mostly from a Buddhist point of view, of these questions, and some (tentative) responses I and others have formulated along the way.

Several summers ago, I attended Naropa Institute in Boulder, Colorado. Founded by the late Chogyam Trungpa, Rinpoche, Naropa saw itself as "the only North American college whose educational philosophy is rooted in the Buddhist contemplative tradition. Contemplative education is education in which the rigor of academic and artistic discipline is balanced by the cultivation of meditative awareness."[2] As it happened, a facility for constructing nuclear weapons was located at Rocky Flats, outside of Boulder. In August, a number of protesters converged in Boulder to commemorate the bombings of Hiroshima and Nagasaki by demonstrating at Rocky Flats. Many Naropa students had come of age in the 1960's and, closely attuned (we thought) to the tenor of the times, had cultivated the political consciousness growing out of the rights, anti-war, and environmental movements. When Trungpa, Rinpoche, was asked about the advisability of participating in the Rocky Flats demonstration, and perhaps engaging in non-violent civil disobedience, he responded: "There's a bigger bomb waiting to go off inside you."

To many Naropa students and practitioners of meditation, including me, this seemed an unsatisfying response: apparent quiescence, even acquiescence, in the face of potential ecocide and genocide, undue capitulation to the existing "power without." If we stuck rigorously to Trungpa's dictum, however cryptic, wouldn't we be accused of the self-centeredness so many critics were seeing in the "spiritual counterculture?"

But for Trungpa and other teachers, non-involvement, rather than being an exercise in narcissism, was really just the reverse: a means by which to allow the ego to remain free of the seduction of belief systems and the constrictions they imposed on consciousness. The essential partiality of belief systems and the dualistic categories they established lead to self-justifying actions based in high-minded notions of exclusion. According to Trungpa, "the most fully developed products of this tendency are ideologies, the systems of ideas that rationalize, justify and sanctify our lives. Nationalism, communism, existentialism, Chris-tianity, Buddhism--all provide us with identities, rules of action, and interpretations of how and why things happen as they do."[3] Thus, involvement growing out of the descriptions, prescriptions, and rationalizations of ideologized belief--including, potentially, Buddhism-- only solidified conceptions of self while circumscribing the cultivation of spaciousness, mindfulness, and compassion.

More recently, I watched on television news a demonstration in San Francisco that responded to a Reagan Administration policy in Central America. The demonstrators advocated the policy position that made the most moral and political sense to me. But then, somehow, a city policeman found himself isolated with the demonstrators in what appeared to be the lobby of a municipal building. Suddenly, they physically attacked him, pummeling and kicking in mob-like fashion. At that point, though not earlier, I could see the wisdom of Trungpa's teaching. While it could be argued that the incident was atypical and, besides, probably distorted by the television context, I am not sure that matters.

If compassion entails the recognition and expression of other people's essential humanness and the spiritual equality of all beings, then the absence of this quality of mind is brutally manifest in the major political, social and economic struggles which dominate the global news, especially those in which the most righteous (often religious) claims are asserted. Perhaps more than any other dynamic, what characterizes these conflicts is the overarching need for there to be *enemies*. The recent work of philosopher Sam Keen is devoted to the insight that "generation after generation we find excuses to hate and dehumanize each other, and we always justify ourselves with the most mature sounding political rhetoric. And we refuse to admit the obvious. We human beings are *Homo hostilis*, the hostile species, the enemy-making animal."[4]

The point is that if, in pursuit of political and social justice, we find only the despised shadow "to bear the burden of our denied enmity,"[5] then neither social justice nor spiritual awakening can result. Instead we continue the dualistic dance of self and other. As Vietnamese Buddhist master, Thich Nhat Hanh, asks, "Where is our enemy?...We still think that the enemy is the other, and that is why we cannot really see him."[6]

For Thich Nhat Hanh and other exponents of "engaged Buddhism," however, compassion is the cutting edge of social action. In fact, compassion, in this view, *requires* a form of activism in the face of the critical problems of the world today. Living and suffering through the devastation of Vietnam and its people led Hanh to conclude that "seeing the suffering leads to compassion. Compassion, in Buddhism, is also basic. If you have compassion, you are not afraid to act; awareness and compassion will certainly lead to action."[7] Similarly, for Christopher Titmuss, a vipassana meditation teacher: "The world is in crisis. How can an awakened mind ignore this brutal fact: Compassion is not a feeling, but is direct, skillful action. Compassionate politics is the politics of protest."[8]

While these views may appear to be disparate with those of Trungpa, I think there is a more important, unifying thread: the quality of mind by which we perceive the world, conditioning the kind of beings we are, shapes the motivations behind and effectiveness of our actions or potential actions. Thus, the critical relationship is among *seeing*, *being*, and *acting*, not in linear progression but as aspects of each other.

* * * * * * * * *

In order for political involvement not to degenerate into "another part of the drama of aggression and fear,"[9] what appears now to be the dichotomy between spiritual quietism and social activism must be reconciled. The "model of integration" (Figure 1) is an attempt to understand how meditative action, rooted in spiritual beliefs and practice is *not* antithetical to or inconsistent with social action, based in political beliefs and practice. What is shown is the possibility of reconciling the antagonism between proponents of individual change (which, to others, at times seems self-centered or narcissistic) and those who seek remedies

54

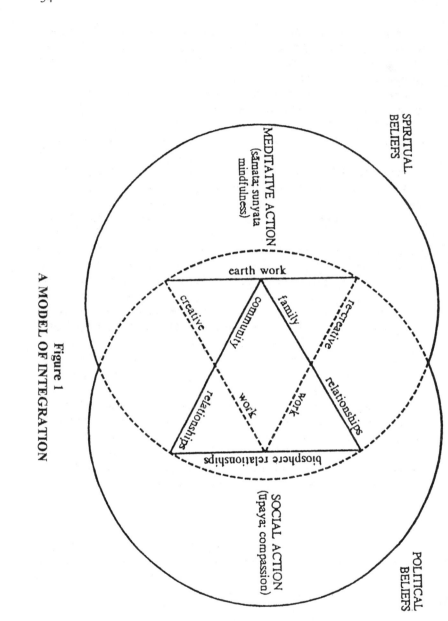

Figure 1
A MODEL OF INTEGRATION

to large social and political problems by attempting to transform institutions or, perhaps, restructure society. In the workshops and retreats he leads and participates in, teacher and psychotherapist Jack Kornfield gives heightened emphasis to the relationship between spiritual and social and political action.

The model suggests that the basis of individual and social transformation is the kind of *work* we do and the nature of the *relationships* we have. Thus, personal and political action revolve around the quality of *how* we see ourselves and *what* we do in the most fundamental aspects of our lives. And there is a balanced, interlocking combination of work and relationship.

Focusing on work and relationship underscores the essential *activist* thrust of this integrative model. Work, in this sense, is best understood as an aspect of *sadhana*, or spiritual practice: "The way we work represents our consciousness--it is the way we manifest our inner being."[10] The fundamental role of work as an expression of our being becomes an inherently political consideration, for non-Marxists as well as Marxists, when the degradation of work in contemporary life is acknowledged. Debasing the creative, recreative, playful and productive elements of the work experience is thus spiritually as well as economically debilitating. The Buddhist noble path of "right livelihood," in this context, entails providing grist for the spiritual mill as well as engaging in creative and compassionate work that is uplifting to others and oneself. While meditation is essential to cultivating concentration and insight, "wisdom and understanding have to be integrated into our lives. Right livelihood is an important part of the integration."[11]

Work as a reflection of one's quality of mind is a concomitant of the development of "skillful means" (ūpaya). Skillful means involves having the clarity of perception to take the appropriate action at a given moment. In a society where work may not only be drudgery but also might cause suffering to others, the consciousness created through skillful means can be subversive. Refusing to engage in work that involves killing or the planning of killing, polluting, or deceiving is actively political and may affect a society's collective conditioning.[12] This, after all, was the central teaching of Gandhi.

One's connectedness with the collectivity is an inescapable facet of life. Integration within the life of the community, the larger culture, and the natural world is a function of the quest for harmony and balance. From a Buddhist point of view, the notion of "sangha," or spiritual community, is integral to achieving that harmony and balance. Sangha may be the means by which the community not only engages in collective meditative action, but also "action in the world," social action grounded in a spiritual perspective.[13]

Poet and Zen practitioner, Gary Snyder, suggests that, in our cultural context, the value of community is largely unappreciated. For Buddhists, sangha should be seen as equally important as the person of the Buddha and his teachings (dharma). An understanding of sangha leads to a fuller appreciation of community, generally, and allows a more expansive perception of relationships to people and to the natural world. For Snyder,

> *There are many levels of sangha. The sangha in one sense is fellow practitioners and the priesthood. In another sense, it's the whole community, it's the watershed, it's the farmers over there, and it's merchants over there. And then, in the larger sense, it's all of humanity, and then in a larger sense, it's all of nature.*[14]

Snyder draws our attention, then, to the interdependence and interconnectedness of our relationships--"how we serve each other"[15]-- and the inherently activist stance in the world underpinning these relationships. Even the large-scale nature of this perception does not mean there isn't the necessity to take action in the moment, in the face of oppression, destruction and confusion. To act, with the understanding of our relation to others, is "a perfectly natural response that actually grows out of dharma practice. Practice leads you to the point where you don't hesitate in the matter of right action when presented with an immediate choice."[16]

* * * * * * * * * *

In an age of possible nuclear war, mass starvation, and continuing ecological destruction, the conflict between advocates of spiritual and political action, "the power within and the power without," can be reconciled. On the one hand, the warnings of spiritual teachers that we only bring more confusion to already polarized political situations when we act out of fear and aggression are important understandings. The human propensity for mythologizing "the enemy" and ideologizing categories of good and evil is apparent. And therefore to label these teachings as narcissistic is to miss the point.

On the other hand, however, meditative action and political action can be seen as aspects of each other. From a Buddhist perspective, meditative practice opens the possibility of understanding the mind and "the forerunner of social action in Buddhist tradition is the understanding of mind...Whatever action is taken must be seen primarily as a part of one's sadhana or spiritual practice."[17] Just as deepening practice enhances the capacity for skillful means, so can social action be a vehicle for precisely that deepening practice. As noted, the life and work of Gandhi were devoted to that understanding. In our own time, so is the compassionate service of Mother Theresa and Ram Dass.

Social and political involvement are concomitants of one's quest for awakening and the awakening of others. The deepening of spiritual practice allows the insight that we are not separate selves; rather, we are inextricably connected with all beings and the life process itself and this, too, allows for the cultivation of a compassionate social action. The pivotal and exquisite role in Buddhism of the bodhisattva, who forgoes nirvana in order to act in the service of the enlightenment of all beings, makes the Mahayana tradition essentially activist and communal.

I have suggested that the *work* we do and the *relationships* we share are "meditation in action" in the world. They allow for right action and communal solidarity to manifest as a social/political stance rooted in mindfulness. They might be seen as the balance points where meditative and political action merge. A centered, quiet mind is empty (sanskrit: sunyata) of solidified conceptions and therefore of projections onto others of undesired qualities, and of rationalizations or ideologies. At the same time, this leads to the development of skillful means (ūpaya), the ability to see "what's happening" and take the appropriate action in all circumstances. And since the essence of a healthy, balanced life is engaging in right livelihood and nourishing relationships, one is always interested in and aware of what is going on.

People who are clear about the need for peace; clean air and water and a healthful food supply; social and economic justice; good schools for children; artistry, craftsmanship, and work that is not degraded;--might, when necessary, engage in such action as boycotts or non-violent civil disobedience after carefully assessing their motivations and likely effects. For these people, then, political life and spiritual life are aspects of the same thing: a quest for wholeness that requires balance and integration. As Benedictine monk and Zen student, Brother David Steindl-Rast, acknowledges: "The great issues of our time always have a spiritual side. You can't separate the two anyway: what is spiritual and what is not spiritual."

NOTES

1. Rexroth, K. "On Flower Wreath Hill." In *The Morning Star*. New York, New Directions, 1979, p. 43.
2. Naropa Institute, *Summer Bulletin*. Boulder, Colarado, 1988, p. 3.
3. Trungpa, C. *Cutting Through Spiritual Materialism*. Boulder, Colorado, Shambala, 1973, p. 6.

58

4. Keen, S. *Faces of the Enemy: Reflections of the Hostile Imagination.* New York, Harper and Row, 1986, pp. 10-11.
5. *Ibid.*
6. Hanh, T. N. "Please Call Me by My True Names." In Eppsteiner, F. and Maloney, D. *The Path of Compassion.* Buffalo, New York, White Pine Press, 1985, p. 75.
7. Gates, B. ed. "Suffering Is Not Enough: An interview with Thich Nhat Hanh." *Inquiring Mind.* Berkeley, California, Summer 1986, p. 11.
8. Titmuss, C. "Western Vipassana Teachers Forum." *Inquiring Mind.* Berkeley, California, Summer 1986, p. 6.
9. Kornfield, J. "Buddhism and Nuclear Politics." In *Co-Evolution Quarterly: Journal for the Protection of All Beings.* Sausalito, California, Fall 1978, p. 30.
10. Tulku, T. *Skillful Means.* Berkeley, California, Shambala, 1978, p. 18.
11. Goldstein, J. *The Experience of Insight: A Natural Unfolding.* Santa Cruz, California, Unity Press, 1976, p. 12.
12. For a discussion of "collective karma," see Kapleau, P. *Zen: Dawn in the West.* Garden City, New York, Anchor/Doubleday, 1980, pp. 251-53.
13. Kornfield, J. *Op. Cit.*, p. 32.
14. Snyder, G. "Chan on Turtle Island." *Inquiring Mind.* Berkeley, California, Winter 1988, p. 5.
15. *Ibid.*
16. *Ibid.*
17. *Ibid.*

Community College Teaching as "Lifework:"
Voice, Experience, and the Evocation of Self

The following essay stems from a much larger qualitative study entailing the "lifework" of community college teaching written in the early 1990s. Community colleges are known and valued primarily as teaching institutions. Most often this translates into an emphasis on pedagogical methods and outcomes, and a de-emphasis of publishing. Rarely explored, however, is the deeper *meaning* of teaching for community college faculty.

I undertook to delve into that meaning by interviewing many of my colleagues from a multiplicity of disciplines at Ulster County Community College, especially concerning how they found what I called their "teaching voices." This study turned into narratives and dialogues involving the discovery and evolution of "teaching voice," defined by one faculty member as "the evocation, even the epiphany, of self...Our teaching is our poetry, our song." Voice emerges from and gives form to authentic experience.

Teaching voice, then, is not so much expressed as *lived*, and inseparable from the whole lives of teachers. Teaching, like poetry, is a form of what Olney calls "lifework"; the study and narration of teaching as experience are therefore more anthropological and autobiographical than pedagogical.

As the continual, often-dramatic, enactment and re-creation of self, community college teaching lifework unfolds only through dialogue and connection with students. In turn, students' voices are activated and resonate as well. Thus, teachers' quest for heightened self-awareness and wholeness is relational, communal and ultimately shared. The shared teaching and learning quest adds another, deeper layer to the meaning of community and provides a fuller understanding of the essential nature and value of community colleges.

* * * * * * * * * *

Teaching, Transmission, and Community

One of my teaching colleagues attempted to further define and elaborate the idea of "voice" by stating the following:

If what you teach transforms your own life and your students see that, then they will believe you... And if you show them that you have been influenced to become more wise, more caring, more communitarian, more loving, more aware, more mindful, even

60

more civilized or more cultured, or educated, and that you manifest that in your own being, then they listen to your voice, then you have a voice.--B.S.

B.S. shows that if a teacher is making some progress in his or her life, then students will pay more attention to what teachers have to offer. Anthropologist Mary Catherine Bateson (1990) subtitles a recent study of the lives of prominent women, "life as a work in progress," a continual coming to oneself.

The teaching life can be seen as a work in progress not only through the always-unfinished connections to students, but also by virtue of how these connections are links with our own teachers. A teacher, like a poet or other artist, is part of a chain of transmission--a passing on--of ideas or artifacts. This enlarges voice, identity and the meaning of "community" for faculty and students of community colleges. "No poet, no artist of any art," wrote T.S. Eliot (1952), "has his complete meaning alone. His significance, his appreciation is the appreciation of his relation to the dead poets and artists. You cannot value him alone; you must set him, for contrast and comparison, among the dead. I mean this as a principle of aesthetic, not merely historical criticism" (p.4). Many of the teachers I interviewed understood and expressed, directly or implicitly, this sense of appreciation and relation.

For philosophy professor, T.D., the chain extends back through his personal mentor into the farther reaches of the history of philosophy and religion. His voice literally is infused with the spirit of the great thinkers and the largeness of their vision. At times, he said, he experiences them speaking *through* him, in such a way as to give substance to "the idea that you can be the voice of humanity." He explained:

I don't mean that in a grandiose way, but a humble way: to speak, as an instrument, for all those who have gone before you; you're now their tongue. You can be the tongue of Plato or Aristotle, to make them still live, because the fact that they're gone in one way does not make them not alive. They're alive and well as long as we can speak.

For T.D., the inspiration for seeing "human beings as having a special role of speaking for history, speaking for nature, speaking in a big way," comes from his own teacher, the late philosopher, Robert Pollock. T.D. prepares meticulously for each class, no matter how many times he has taught a course, and often he will mentally confer with Pollock before teaching a class. In that way, T.D. acts as a conduit, a channel, for the expansiveness of vision and voice to flow from his mentor to his students.

And in a real way, T.D. asks for his teacher's blessing, and wants not to let him down:

> *Even though I thought Pollock was brilliant, he always said -- and took it seriously--that he wasn't that smart, but was a good receiver, a good channel. He had good receptors, good antennae; that's the way he saw himself, like a good artist or philosopher. My antennae are small compared to those of Nietzsche or even Pollock, but to have good antennae is to be receptive to those things that are there. You know, in this mental preparation before class, I try to put my antennae up, and I ask him to kind of be with me. And I guess that's participating in that tradition. Also, I don't want to fail him. I don't want to disappoint him.*

In the Zen Buddhist tradition there is a chant by which practitioners of *zazen* (meditation) pay homage to the venerable masters in their lineage through whom the great understandings of zen have been transmitted to current teachers and students. The chant begins with the leader saying: "O Awakened Ones! May the power of your Samadhi sustain" (Zen Center, 1975, p.12). The practitioners then chant the names, followed by "honored one," of the great masters in the lineage, the patriarchal line. At the conclusion of the chant, the leader says, "You who have handed down the light of Dharma, we shall repay your benevolence" (p.14).

One of my colleagues, W.S., who teaches business and has extensive corporate experience (and, coincidentally, is a Buddhist) tells a moving story from his learning and teaching life that, at once, is a "repayment of benevolence" and underscores the transpersonal quality of teaching experience. He recounted how a returning student who had been away from school for several years was experiencing difficulty in the conceptual part of a computer course, even though he was familiar with computers through his work as a landscaper. As the course progressed, the student's struggle intensified until, finally, he wrote a note to W.S. saying he would have to drop the course because of a conflict with his job. "But," according to W.S., "what I sensed was that he had just become overwhelmed and frustrated by it." W.S. then told me that he, too, had experienced difficulty in a course as a student:

> *I took a course several years ago in the bamboo flute, in Berkeley. It was called "beginning bamboo flute," but everyone in the class except for me had played some kind of instrument. Some of them had played silver flutes. So I would go into this course and I could just barely make this little note. And they were playing these wonderful scales, going up and down, and I was hyperventilating into this bamboo flute. Every once in a while*

I'd get a little note. I remember, every week I would go home,
practice like crazy and come back--I remember coming back
being able to play these three little notes, and playing them
fairly well. But when I came back, everyone else had gone way
past me.

W.S. grew extremely discouraged and decided to leave the class for
the term. But the teacher encouraged him to stick it out: "Don't drop out.
They can slow down. They can play just one note. That won't hurt them
at all." W.S. stayed in the class and, ultimately, became proficient at
playing the bamboo flute. Remembering the experience as "a tremendous
kind of gift," W.S. then did the same thing with his student: he called and
asked him to come back to the course, and said he would provide the extra
help necessary to put the student back on track. The man did return to
complete the course, and he and W.S. have had a continuing relationship
over several years. "I tried," W.S. said, "to add some kind of value to his
life, some kind of movement from where he was--which is what education
is." Another way to say it is that W.S., while acting at that moment in
response to what Martin Buber (1958) would call hearing the students
voice as "Thou," was also recreating the generosity bestowed upon him
by his bamboo flute teacher.

For English professor/poet/naturalist/folklorist/and regional historian,
B.S., teaching is also an act of generosity--"that's what the greatest
teaching is, a gift"--to be transmitted from one's teacher to his students.
When the teaching and learning connection is made, when, as Buber
(1965) said, there is a "turning towards the other," and hearing the
students' voice as "Thou," the lives of teachers and students are changed
profoundly. At the same time, the web of culture and community,
comprised of the shared meanings among teachers and students, is
enlarged. Buber called these connections "the life of dialogue," which
further reveal the inner core of voice (p. 25). B.S.'s teacher is the poet and
environmental activist, Gary Snyder, whom he met and became close with
in 1966 after a poetry reading at a large state university where B.S. then
taught. According to B.S., the world, and therefore his life, transformed
irreversibly:

Gary changed my life by changing how I saw the world; he
stopped the world for me. That's what a great teacher does: he
stops the world. That's it: he presents a new world to you--and
it's pretty scary. And if, beyond stopping the world, he can
present a new world; if he can, metaphorically, replace aspects
of the old world with new ones, then there's no going back.

Snyder taught B.S. Zen meditation, the spiritual and psychological as
well as ecological significance of wilderness, and the importance of

making a commitment to a place and its people ("digging in"). The meeting and subsequent relationship with Snyder convinced B.S. and his wife it was important for them to "come home" to the Hudson River Valley and Southern Catskill Mountain region of New York State, where they grew up. For B.S., teaching at a community college--as well as living in, writing about, and exploring the larger (including wild) community--has been an essential aspect of his digging in. B.S. has become-- through his teaching, poetry and other writing, public lectures, and ecoactivism--the foremost interpreter of regional life in our area. "But," he told me, "when I say in one of my poems 'all things holy here,' I wouldn't have known that without meeting Gary."[1]

One of the things Gary presented to me was a coherent view of the world and a thoughtful, mindful way of being in the world: that things made sense, you could understand what was happening, you didn't have to be just acted upon. If you could understand the nature of things, you could act. That measure of mindfulness and control was something I had no idea about previously.

As B.S. and many of my community college colleagues attest, great teachers, real teachings, true education are not so much about descriptions of the world, but living and acting in it. They afford authenticity, identity, and agency--in a word, voice. Critical to the voice I was finding in my earliest teaching years was my coming upon a teacher who, as Snyder did for B.S., would alter how I saw the world and wanted, at least then, to be in the world. He is Jonathan Kozol, the teacher, author, and social critic. I had not read, or even heard of, *Death At An Early Age* (1967) when, in the Fall of 1970, a student brought me a tape of a lecture Kozol had recently given in Boston. And I wouldn't come to meet Kozol until I invited him to speak at our college nearly eight years later. But Kozol's understanding of the political indoctrination function of public schools, and his unswerving commitment to racial and social justice were (and continue to be) so powerful, so inspiring, so unshakeable, as to give direction to my own teaching and, in fact, tie my teaching directly to the other parts of my life.

What struck me initially about Kozol was, literally, his voice. In addition to the sheer radicalism of his message--articulating what I had been searching to understand within my own context--I was knocked out by his manner of expression, especially the passion, timbre, and intensity of his anger. It was a voice which, with all its high-pitched stridency and indignation, I would adopt (not always to good effect) unashamedly because of its uncompromising clarity and commitment. It was a voice that compelled me to try to understand the two domains with which I was then immediately concerned--public education and political power--and their interrelation. More than anything, though, it was a voice that demanded teaching be a *lifework* resonating with that clarion call of compassion and *lived* ethical enlistment in the cause of social justice in all aspects of my life. In the time of My Lai, Nixon, and an active Ku Klux Klan in our own county, I believed then, along with Kozol, "we live in the midst of pain and nightmare and injustice" (1974, p.1).

What I learned from Kozol I initially applied to the community college as a critique; but I also came to see, in a positive sense, how the experience and practice of community college teaching as lifework can exemplify what Kozol as well as Snyder had been saying about digging in, finding or creating a field of action, making a commitment to where one is.[2] If, for Kozol (1975), "public school is a 12-year exercise of ethical *emaciation*" (p. 130, emphasis added), I wanted, first, to place the community college within the larger framework of schooling as political socialization, but then to make our college in particular a locus of ethical as well as intellectual *emancipation*. For me, this meant raising questions about the "cooling-out" process of higher education at the two-year level,[3] and the too-close connection between the college and local corporate interests. I felt that the college blew with the political and economic winds, at least in part because it lacked a philosophical and pedagogical mooring beyond the blandest "mission statement." The point is that in the name of a misguided pragmatism, I thought the college in its curriculum and process perpetuated, often implicitly, the kind of ideological instruction at the heart of public schooling.[4]

But, for me, it also meant attempting to create more community focus within the college, and a greater attentiveness to often-ignored constituencies in the larger community the college purported to serve. This gave rise to an intensity of involvement on my part (not always consistent with my more introverted nature) over a number of years with a wide range of political action: working with the local anti-poverty agency, organizing a peace group, helping to found and run a food co-op, serving as a volunteer mediator in family disputes, and heading my town's environmental conservation commission. All of this came back into my courses and, in fact, often involved students outside of class; thus, teaching and the rest of my life had virtually merged, forming a continuum of activism, putting into practice Kozol's sense that "history is not something that is done to you or me. History is made by men and women" (1976).

I think this was effective pedagogy, up to a point. It helped to identify for students and myself some of the key issues of our time and how they are manifest right around us. It also helped to break down the barrier between the college classroom and the "outside world." Over time, though, if Kozol's radical activism and passionate sense of struggle were difficult for me to emulate and sustain, so were mine for my students. If Kozol's anger was, at times, not only a call to action but also a source of despair, so perhaps was mine. I felt that quality of angriness and stridency was not always helpful to the great diversity of students I was meeting in my classes, many of whom were struggling with quite profound and dramatic real-life situations that bred a kind of uninformed, though perhaps intuitively-sound, cynicism I did not want to feed, gratuitously. I hoped, instead, to create a larger context for understanding where their situations may fit, and how, personally and some day professionally, they might be more effective to act relative to those situations.

Also true is that my own life had changed in important ways and I couldn't always carry that anger with me.[5] My voice, therefore, began to change as well; and only when I could step back, with great affection, from the Jonathan Kozol in me could I come to what I heard much more as my own voice. For a good part of the past twenty-five years, that voice, joined with the voices of many of my colleagues, has been more concerned with who students are and what they might become: their level of consciousness, aspiration, and connectedness to what is happening around and within them. This may, and often does, find expression politically or in the larger social framework: I was pleased, last year, when a student, not knowing my "connection" to Kozol, brought his most recent book on education, *Savage Inequalities* (1991), to class one night (I hadn't yet read it) and said she now wanted to be a teacher. *Amazing Grace*, set in the South Bronx, has now been published as well, and while Kozol speaks of his depression in the face of being unable to bring political, economic, social and educational change, I can hear the old anger and stridency that especially fuels Kozol's voice.

Thus, with Kozol's help, I have found my own way to exploring with students their lived experience, and mine, turning "self-abdication" into self-affirmation. In the end, through those voices, along with Kozol, we come to realize that "truth" is not a word to be spoken, but "a deed that can be done.... or a word that can be lived" (Goldman, 1975, p.13). Like Gary Snyder for B.S., Kozol, through the example of his own life/teachings, showed me the connection among teaching, being, and acting in the world. Those lives and those teachings are then transmitted to students and, in turn, shape their quest.

Teaching and learning as quest

B.S. is not only the student of Gary Snyder; he is also the author of a highly-acclaimed critical biography of the poet. In the book, *Gary Snyder* (Steuding, 1976), B.S. notes that Snyder, like Thoreau and Pound before him, sees his work and his life as attempts to mythologize experience. Through his art and way of living, Snyder is "seeking personal liberation, the formation of a new social mythology, and, ultimately, the regeneration of society" (p. 68). Snyder's vision, then, is the heroic quest or journey and his poetry is, consciously, giving voice to that vision. B.S. told me:

Snyder was living consistent with his view of the world--that was one of his great teachings. Gary didn't just point the way to another consciousness; through his poems and readings and the way he lives, he was able to make his teachings experiential.

If, indeed, "our teaching is our poetry, our song," I have found that for many community college faculty, teaching as lifework --teaching as autobiographical experience--is also a quest, an often-dramatic artistic and experiential journey with potentially profound personal and social, as well as educational, implications. For those of us who experience it that way, teaching is central to the script of our "personal mythology."[6] Rather than "write" our autobiographies, we *act*, perform, our lives, creating ourselves as the drama unfolds, donning different masks for the ever-changing inner *dramatis personae*, the "internal cast" of who we have been and will become.

T.D. creates a sense of philosophical wonder in his classroom by "becoming" Kant, Hume, and Nietzsche--teaching these thinkers "from the inside out" such so that, when teaching and learning become "living the experience from deep down in the bottom of yourself, you should shake." Psychology professor L.C. "becomes" catatonic, paranoid, on the stage of his classroom--enacting psychoses in all their grandeur and terror and, at the same time, consciously cultivating the capacity for compassion in his students. C.D., the business instructor and former marketing executive, teaches from her feminist perspective the interrelation among family values, women's issues, and "male-dominated corporate America"--while, at this writing, being six months pregnant. J.J.C., dry spittle settled like cotton in the corners of his own cracked lips, reads to a spell-bound class his poem, "The Rainmaker's Boy"--and "becomes" the skinny boy "hag-ridden with fever" who breaks open the clouds and brings down the rain.[7]

"Performance," seen in this way, is not a form of entertainment, but a medium for creating shared felt experience, and thus the vehicle for the connection and relationship that foster and enhance real learning. Teaching as art is not teachers' skillful dissemination or students' successful assimilation of content; rather, it is establishing the *relatedness* and *connectedness* for knowing to occur. In teaching as dramatic performance, as in all art, ultimately performer, subject matter, and audience are one.

In this view, though, students are not passive audience, but co-actors, the creators of their own autobiographies. And thus, the process of teaching and knowing as autobiographical drama inexorably *enfolds* as it *unfolds*: it is quintessentially shared and communal, even while individually transformative. This has important implications because our culture does not provide meaningful guidance for pursuit of individual creative change or the cultivation of positive interdependence and community. And the educational system, as a whole, reflects and fosters the dominant culture's drive toward conformism and atomistic individualism. Robert Bellah, et al (1985), in their now-classic study of "individualism and commitment in American life," describe a society that gives rise to "the self apart from history and community." The lives of American people are often lacking "the kind of story or narrative, as of a pilgrimage or quest, that many cultures have used to link private and public; past, present, and future; and the life of the individual to the life of society and the meaning of the cosmos" (p. 83).

In their own way, many of my colleagues, through the teaching life, against the grain, are attempting to provide that guidance, that cultivation, those stories, for themselves and their students. They are people in quest of a "myth to live by,"[8] who may aid, even launch, others on a quest of their own. They guide students in their search for identity, community, and creative transformation by being seekers themselves.

As teachers enact and work through their own lived experience, so, too, do their students. For those students who brave the path of discovery, the learning quest is often a frightening but ultimately exhilarating and transformative mythic journey inextricably linked to that of their teachers. For J.H., undertaking Ulster County Community College's Honors Program entailed the choice to study that which would inexorably change her life in ways she hadn't anticipated; this meant "taking the conscious journey on the labyrinthine path" and emerging, along with Teilhard de Chardin and philosophy professor T.D., "with the elaboration of ever more perfect eyes within a cosmos in which there is always more to be seen." J.H. realized that, for her, only this path could reveal the potential for insight, growth, change, even wisdom. She concluded:

We are not provided with wisdom; we must discover it for our-
selves, after a journey through a wilderness which no one else

68

can take for us, an effort no one else can spare us, for our wisdom is the point of view from which we come at last to regard this world (p. 13).[9]

Here, too, teachers may act, perform, as guides, through the drama of our own lived experience, for that "journey through the wilderness" we hope our students will risk. Perhaps they will encounter what Gary Snyder (1957) called the "rare and powerful states of mind" embodied by their own voices which then would "sing or speak from authentic experience" (p. 117). Another woman, P.L., who also undertook the journey of the learning quest, sang her experience this way:

Ancient fires
that consumed the saplings
here
have died to a smoky haze--
there will be new life,
soon.[10]

And so, for teachers and students, authentic lived experience--felt, thought, sensed and acted--is the seed-germ of the art, the poetry of the educative process. When the voice, the song, of the teacher resonates clear and true, then students join in and find their voices as well. The result is the mutual infusion of action and vision: the connectedness, relationship, dialogue, and community which emerge from, embody, and define teaching practice.

NOTES

1. See Steuding (1990, p. 95), "Things in Reserve."
2. B.S. and I had often compared, in those earlier days, the radical wilderness and urban visions of Snyder and Kozol, and their respective calls for consistent commitment to place and fields of action. Kozol (1972) wrote of the "need to find one solid core of concrete action and specific dedication in one neighborhood, or in one city, with just one group of allies, and with one set of loyalties, and with one deep dream of love and transformation." See,"Moving on to Nowhere," New York *Times*, March 24, p. 41.
3. See, for example, Clark (1960).
4. See Katims (1973).
5. Among other life changes was my marriage in 1975, and the arrival of our son, Ren, in 1985. In the interim, I had renewed my practice of buddhist, vipassana meditation and was writing and publishing poetry.
6. See Larsen (1990); Larsen is a professor of psychology at Ulster County Community College.

69

7. See Clarke (1981).
8. Campbell (1972).
9. J.H. is soon to complete her undergraduate studies in anthropology at Vassar College.
10. See Law (1987), "Regeneration: By Degree (Graduation)."

REFERENCES

Bellah, R.N., Madsen, R., Sullivan, W.M., Swidler, A., & Tipton, S.M. (1985). *Habits of the Heart: Individualism and Commitment in American Life.* New York: Harper & Row.

Bateson, M.C. (1990). *Composing a life: Life as a work in progress - the improvisations of five extraordinary women.* New York: Penguin Books.

Buber, M. (1958). *I and thou.* New York: Charles Scribner's Sons.

_____. (1965). *Between man and man.* New York: Macmillan.

Campbell, J. (1972). *Myths to live by.* New York: Viking Press.

Clark, B. (May, 1960). The cooling-out function in higher education. *American journal of sociology.* Volume 65.

Clarke, J.J. (1981). *Hagstones.* High Falls, NY: Canal Press.

Eliot, T.S. (1950). Tradition and the individual talent. *Selected Essays, new edition.* New York: Harcourt, Brace, and World.

Goldman, S. (1975). Interview: Jonathan Kozol. *East West Journal.* November 15, 1975, pp. 12-14, 25.

Katims, R. (1973). *The power within/the power without: An inquiry into personal and political sources of transformation.* Unpublished doctoral dissertation, Union Institute, Cincinnati.

Kozol, J. (1967). *Death at an early age: The destruction of the minds and hearts of Negro children.* Boston: Houghton Mifflin.

_____. (1974). Straightforward lies. *Fellowship.* Nyack, NY: The Fellowship of Reconciliation.

_____. (1975). *The night is dark and I am far from home.* Boston: Houghton Mifflin.

_____. (1976). Against the chorus, but for the "movement." *New York Times.* August 1, sec. IV, p.15.

_____. (1991). *Savage Inequalities: Children in America's Schools.* New York: Crown.

Larsen, S. (1990). *The mythic imagination: Your quest for meaning through personal Mythology.* New York: Bantam Books.

Law, P. (1987). *Beginner's mind.* Unpublished paper. Ulster County Community College, Stone Ridge, NY.

Snyder, G. (1957). *Earth house hold.* New York: New Directions.

Steuding, B. (1976). *Gary Snyder.* Boston: Twayne.

70

_____. (1990). *A Catskill Mountain journal*. Fleischmanns, New York: Purple Mountain Press.

Zen Center. (1975). *Daily chants and ceremonies*. Rochester, NY.

The Community College, A "Higher Education," and the Process of Initiation

Not long ago I attended a conference at a State University of New York campus, the concern of which was "The Liberal Arts in a Time of Crisis." A central theme of the conference was the now-familiar dichotomy between the declining liberal arts and the blossoming vocational or career programs.

I was a primary participant on two panels: "The Adult Learner and the Liberal Arts" and "The Vocationalization of the Community College." Each panel raised serious questions about the changing nature of contemporary higher education; but both, I felt, lacked a certain vitality because of their failure to confront some fundamental considerations which, these days, are buried in the practical sweep of education and its new language of "marketing" and "student-consumers." And while there was a measure of respect accorded the place and function of community colleges in the higher education scheme of things, especially in regard to adult learners, I came to realize that there is a misperception as to what often occurs among *and within* our students. One participant, for example praised community colleges because he saw them as places in which students are "at low risk." For reasons discussed below, I think that for a significant number of community college students, this is--and should be--profoundly untrue.

The discussion that follows is an attempt to rediscover, in the context of contemporary college practice, the psychosocial process of "initiation." Since initiation, properly understood, has always served the dual educational functions of shaping individual identity while fostering social continuity, my aim is to raise questions and considerations about the role played by higher education institutions, especially community colleges, in this process. These include:

- How does the initiatory process relate to the structure and goals of higher education?
- If, as most observers acknowledge, rituals of initiation are absent or obscure in our society, can a college be a source of revitalizing the initiatory experience?
- If initiation *can* be a function of higher education, is there a qualitatively unique role for community colleges, especially in view of the nature of their student bodies?

In my view, then, the question for higher education is *not* so much how do we win students back to the liberal arts, but how do we underscore the college's role as a vehicle for personal transformation and a truly higher learning? And therefore, any "crisis" in higher education is only tangential to the liberal arts. The crisis, if indeed one exists, has to do with the perception of the function of the college. It has to do with what we would like to see happen within that context and what kind of people we would like to see emerge.

* * * * * * * * * *

What is initiation and how does it relate to the structure and goals of higher education? Every society, in order to achieve integration and continuity, must have some process by which people discover a personal sense of self and its relation to the social structure as a whole. We know, for example, that most primitive and traditional societies have well-defined procedures to effect the transition from childhood to adulthood. The Zuni Kachina ceremonies and the vision quest of American Plains Indians groups are only two of the better known examples of *rites de passage*. Anthropologists, psychologists and serious students of all societies stress the importance of these rituals, which are the dramatic counterpart to a society's mythology, in providing guides for the quest towards psychospiritual well-being and social orientation. And in recent years, the necessity for "passages" at all critical junctures of people's lives, not just puberty, has become apparent.

A ritual of initiation, operating within a mythological framework and taking place at various life stages, functions as a vehicle for identity clarification, communal solidarity, and what might be called "creative transformation." Joseph Campbell, the eminent mythologist, indicates that these rituals give form to human life in a profound and substantial way: they help to shape and raise to awareness the natural changes a developing person undergoes--changes in being, status, and relation to others. The rites of passage and other rituals of transformation serve, therefore, both a psychological and a sociological function. They are trials and ordeals in their most basic meaning and, at bottom, are primarily educational. So critical are these functions that historian of religion, Mircea Eliade, concludes, "Initiation lies at the core of any genuinely human life."[1]

Sensitive observers have long recognized the absence, or at least the muted nature of an integrated mythological and ritualistic structure in the modern Western world. C. G. Jung spoke of "modern man in search of a soul," indicating the lack of such a frame in general and the failure of Christianity in particular. Others, especially those concerned with art and literature, have joined in searching for or creating a "new" myth, what Mark Schorer in his study of William Blake calls the "hunt for the essential image."

If, for modern technological societies, particularly our own, the ritual experiences and supporting mythological frame are obscure (or even non-existent), what are the implications for contemporary institutions, especially those of higher learning? One important response is that schooling on all levels becomes an instrument of bureaucratic processing rather than personal transformation:

In our day education has ceased to be a preparation for initiation; it has lost its true function of a training for inner maturity by a tempering of the will. Answers are given, information injected, instead of a channel opened to receive knowledge and an instrument prepared to re-express it, usually...the instrument is spoiled instead of attuned by schooling.[2]

Ironically, Ivan Illich and other critics have suggested that educational institutions comprise in industrialized societies a kind of secular church, whose "clergy" and rites operate largely in the service of dominant elites and their ideologies. For Illich, "school is a ritual of initiation which introduces the neophyte to the sacred race of progressive consumption, a ritual of propitiation where academic priests mediate between the faithful and the gods of privilege and power."[3] The function of education, in this view, is chauvinistic, and schools, including colleges, indoctrinate students into the cultural symbology intended to produce social continuity and acceptable, i.e., nonthreatening, patterns of behavior. But there is a world view of difference between this kind of chauvinism and the potential for the integration of the individual with the collective roots of society--the function of meaningful initiation.

The questions arising out of the discussion to this point are: can college revitalize the initiatory function, and if so, what kind of context is necessary for this revitalization? Finally, what unique role can community colleges play in this regard?

College can, I think, be a context for initiatory transformation, not merely as a random sidelight to what is generally conceived to be the "real work," but as an integral and essential condition within the process of education. I have been arguing that initiation is not simply a frivolous diversion from, but is *central* to, a real education. In fact, in my view, a genuine higher learning is incomplete without the quality of change that takes place, as a conscious endeavor, through ritual passage. At present, however, the structure and expressed goals of college education present the initiatory process as an obscure or superfluous underside to the important, more practical purposes for being in school. Yet colleges, including community colleges, continue to advance the *rhetoric* of individual identity, communal solidarity, and creative insight as primary

74

objectives. Noting the value of initiation within the college environment, Professor Jay Williams has remarked:

> In a word, a college should not aim to be another more or less pleasant link in a continuous pathway between cradle and grave. College should be a time for short-circuiting and tearing down, for the fearful and painful experience of tumbling bodily into deep water. Only then can it also be a time of building and planting, creating a new person, swimming joyfully in water 60 fathoms deep.[4]

The potential for developing the insights inherent to the initiatory experience may exist within the framework of the community college. The nature of the community college and the students it attracts present a unique opportunity to fill the initiatory void. Although the community college has been the subject of extensive, often negative commentary, especially concerning social stratification and equal opportunity, there is a core of people who, consciously or unconsciously, look to and find in the community colleges precisely the experience found in initiation. This is especially true of many nontraditional students, often women, who come to the community college after years of being away from formal education. Some examples from my own recent experience are illustrative.

A bright and personable woman who was taking one of my classes came into my office one morning. I could see that she was upset, and the pretense that she used to begin the conversation was quickly dropped. She perceived that her problem was, in a sense, political and, because I was her political science instructor, sought me out. It became apparent, however, that what was bothering her went deeper than the issue she raised. And, in some measure, she was not unique among my students.

Wilma had been a secretary in a public school, but increasingly "felt deadened" by what she came to experience as the dullness of her job. She quit when she was told by the school principal that she did not deserve a raise because, as a married woman, she was only working for "pin money," ostensibly to supplement her husband's income. Now in her late thirties, Wilma decided to come to the community college, in defiance of her husband who is a correction officer, because she "wanted more." Their children were now more independent, and one daughter was already in college. Wilma wanted to study social work.

The combination of twenty years away from school, a skeptical husband, and competition with her daughter for grades created extensive pressure for Wilma. When she came to me, she was trying to deal with her husband's contempt for her changing political consciousness. Her husband, for example, had been opposed to the Equal Rights Amendment, she said, because if the ERA was so controversial there must have been something wrong with it.

Clearly, contrary to the often-stated assumption that adults entering community colleges "are at low risk," Wilma's experience indicates the risk-filled situation she chose to engage and struggle within. She was, in short, "tumbling in deep water."

More recently I spoke with another woman, Lesley, who had just graduated from Ulster County Community College. She is a mother of three and has been physically disabled since birth. She was transferring to a four-year SUNY college and aspired to graduate degrees. She said, however, that before coming to the community college:

I did nothing for fifteen years, and I thought I was going crazy. I went to psychiatrist after psychiatrist, but no one knew what was wrong with me. What was wrong was that I have this fine mind in a body that's not worth a damn, and I was vegetating.

I was a good mother, but I had no hope, and I couldn't teach my children hope. Now I have it, and can teach them. My parents didn't understand education for its own sake. They saw it only as a means to a better job, and that wasn't relevant to me.

Besides, I have to struggle for the next generation [of disabled people]. In the next generation, they will be seen as a natural part of a college. But if we don't do it now, they will have to fight later on.[5]

The creative thrust of successful initiation also entails a transformation of the self that is often expressed as a kind of rebirth. And, for Patricia, another student, who returned to college in her mid-thirties and has, with great courage, taken the path of creative transformation. Patricia became a fine poet and caretaker of children as her own sense of self became more expansive.

For all three women, then, the community college became the alchemical crucible for the quest of precisely those qualities of experience that initiation helps to uncover: an altered identity, a sense of communal solidarity, and a heightened creative potential. Their insights and concerns surely are not just practical or merely academic. They are psychological, social, and if you will, spiritual in nature.

But the need for this level of understanding is there for students of all ages, and both sexes, in college for a variety of reasons. One day, in the gymnasium, I had the chance to speak with a young student who was having difficulties at college. After a semester, he was undecided as to whether to "major" in business or political science. The young man related that a business instructor had told him of a former student who was making a substantial income selling computer cash registers. At the same time, however, he was enticed by the excitement he sensed in politics and wanted "to do something to help people." This young student's problem was not simply vocational. He was wrestling as well with how he sees himself and wants to present that self to the world.

In this context, the meaning of "vocation" changes and a college performs only limited service simply to help students select courses and assess the job market. Expressing the aims of a humanistic education, Abraham Maslow has argued that "the chief goals of the ideal college...would be the discovery of identity, and with it the discovery of vocation."[6] But it may be that community colleges, in attempting to fulfil these goals in some way have, at times, unduly equated "occupation" and "career" with "vocation." Vocation might be more properly understood as a calling centered in a growing sense of self, whereby, according to Williams, "what matters is purpose, concern, and commitment, not so much for the future as for now. It is more important to *be* than to be *something*...."[7]

* * * * * * * * * *

Can these somewhat abstract, philosophical goals be effected for large numbers of students of all ages within the context of a realistic college curriculum with its increasingly practical focus, especially when the language of human potential has been relegated to the "excesses of the 1960's" or co-opted into "leadership training (i.e., management) courses? I think so.

The experience of initiation integrated within any meaningful college curriculum demands not only basic literacy--the ability to think well and clearly, and the ability to articulate what one thinks and believes--but careful inculcation of the tools of understanding so that one can *act* effectively as well.

Emphasizing the initiatory function of education implies, therefore, not only traditional study, but active *engagement* and *relationship*--and being put to the test by those who have already come through and understand the process. President Leon Botstein of Bard College has, in this regard, spoken of education as the development of the "capacity for common discourse," whereby students engage in political, social and moral dialogue not as an act of gentility, but as an expression of learning that is decisive for survival.[8]

The level of survival becomes more fully known through a vision in which the psychosocial characteristics that, at present, are dormant in our society are reawakened. That vision accompanies the process of initiation. A real education is consistent with initiation when it is a catalyst for fully-authentic individuals to function in a social world where that authenticity and individuality are both honored and needed.

NOTES

1. Quoted by D. M. Dooling, "Focus," *Parabola*, Spring 1976, p. 1.
2. *Ibid.*
3. Illich, I. *Deschooling Society.* New York: Harper and Row, 1971, p. 44.
4. Williams, J. G. "The Ritual of Initiation: Implications for the Liberal Arts," *Educational Record*, Vol. 63, No. 1, Winter 1982, p. 30.
5. From a personal communication, October 4, 1985. Quoted with permission.
6. Maslow, A. *The Farther Reaches of Human Nature*. New York: Viking, 1971, p. 183.
7. Williams, *op.cit.*
8. From an address by Leon Botstein, "College Could Be Worth It," SUNY College at New Paltz, January 31, 1981.

About the Author

Rich Katims is Professor of Political Science at Ulster Community College, where he has taught since 1969. He holds degrees from Queens College, CUNY, the American University, and a Ph.D. from the Union Institute. Katims is a recipient of the State University of New York Chancellor's Award for Excellence in Teaching and a University of Texas Master Teacher Award. His poems, essays and political commentaries have appear in *Wordsmith, Waterworks, Insight, Colleague*, the *Interface Journal*, the *Woodstock Times*, and the *Poughkeepsie Journal*. A chapbook of poems *Dragon Kite* was published in 1979.

An activist in community affairs, Katims has served on the Boards of Directors of Family of Woodstock, the Ulster Literacy Association, Ulster County Community Action, and President of the High Falls Food Coop. He has led book and topical discussion groups for inmates at the Eastern New York Correctional Facility, and served as a volunteer mediator with the Mediation Center of Dutchess County.

Katims is a two-time Ulster County Senior Men's Tennis Champion as well as the winner of eight other singles and doubles tournaments. Part of his pleasure includes supporting youth sports programs. He coached Little League baseball and basketball in the Town of Olive, and American Youth Soccer Organization teams in the Town of Marbletown.

Rich Katims lives in Olivebridge NY with his wife Ide and their son Ren, who is a 14 year old freshman at the Onteora High School. Ide Katims is Associate Professor of Nursing at SUNY New Paltz and, most recently, served for several years as Director of undergraduate and graduate programs for the Nursing Department. *Soundings* was designed and produced by Ide Katims, and is thus wholly a collaboration between Ide and Rich Katims to allow the work to appear.